a pressed wafer book

john thompson   **poems   trainride elsewhere**

ISBN 978-1-940396-19-4
First Edition
Printed in the United States of America

PRESSED WAFER
375 Parkside Avenue, Brooklyn, NY 11226
www.pressedwafer.com

Coup de hache

She killed a snake with the hoe.

However harmless,
we want them away from the house. The snake was
big for a garter and it bled

fiercely the more she hit at it. After, she washed
the cold blood off the doorstep. She was shaken

enough as she dropped it in the burn-barrel she
said she heard

voices

Guy Birchard
Further than the Blood
(Boston: Pressed Wafer, 2010)

dedication

to the wonderful and almighty Fanny Howe! you took a
chance when no one else would & wrote back! without you
i'd still be in the hopes and dreams phase! thank you! you
will always have my gratitude!

thank you Chris Scarber for reading the thousands of
poems i've written & hanging in through the bombardment.
you will always be with me good friend!

to my mom, aelena thompson, who did the cover. her
phenomenal photography is inspiring! i thank you for your
talents, courage, and power with the push i always needed.

contents

introduction

In 2012 a letter arrived from a stranger, with the address
of a prison: his name, his number, and the address: Prison
Connector Road in Kentucky. He had read my poetry and
he wanted me to read his. Whatever got him into trouble
was never fully revealed in the months after we began
writing to each other. He didn't complain too much but was
consistent in letting me know how much time he had left
to serve. He ended up in solitary from time to time, and he
spoke of his mother who would get books to him.

He had read lots of contemporary poems, many in *Poetry*
magazine, and had managed to follow further the poets
he admired. His mind was his library. He had no access to
internet and depended entirely on people responding to his
letters and sending him work, and his mother. He is very
young, in his mid-twenties at most, and is burning with
love for boys and men like him, one still in prison now, his
favorite, who he says he will marry when they are both free.

He is out now, living at home and learning to type on a
computer and dig into its mines for poetry and everything
else.

His name is John Thompson, and after I had read about
three batches of his poems, I sent them to Bill Corbett of
Pressed Wafer to read. They were all handwritten in large
circular letters bending a little backward, on lined paper
with ink. Bill immediately saw what I saw, which was "the
real thing"—a mental rhythm and an emotional tone that
emerged as one complete figure. Intimate, vulnerable.

I managed to get through to him a volume of John
Wieners' poems, and Bill began sending him more books

and chapbooks, and has since done a broadside of a few of John's poems and spoken to him at his home in Kentucky. John continues to write to me, eagerly and with delight in his own work and others he has come upon; he writes so often I can hardly keep up with him.

I have been prepared by his prison time to know him only through his poems, which is for me the point of reading poetry anyway: to get the news, so to speak, on paper. The news both exotic and ordinary, wild and thoughtful, the news that carries us to a place unknown, a private place hidden in the middle of America. This volume of poems has come to us from such a place and we are lucky to have it in hand during our own *trainride elsewhere*.

Fanny Howe
January 5, 2016

part one

trainride elsewhere

felicity

you sit in the chair.
i'm cross-legged on the floor
at an acute angle.

ex parte

you lie in bed:

there,
swollen,

your leg
teeters on edge;

your foot
a serene
pendulum;

you are open.

there are traces
of last night
everywhere.

convivial

my mind
transpires
    to softened butter

my features are churned
to transparency

& smear
to obscurity: my brain is bruised

i skin
the membrane to reveal

the innards
    of self: occupy

visualize

come to me

there are the trees that have the leaves
that absorb the spirits
which bloom faces along their branches

the curve of light that glints in the eyes
listen to the ripple, a wave on the sea
that crashes into the eyelash

a fish burrows under the pupil
the threads in the iris begin to unravel
there is a nakedness underneath

that is underdeveloped, that i hide
i scratch off his name on the stone
why is he there, he is not there

he has come to me like a dream
like a bombing, all at once, fast
i cannot comprehend the warmth of sheets

a whitewash painted across my body
a galaxy that is somewhere in the universe
as gone as a falling leaf

the coming

the sun is cooling, nevertheless,
snow has yet to fall

a fresh flame brews inside the stomach of metal walls—

i know
winter is coming but it only touches me
in sleep.

the frozen flakes
like fingertips
play the piano across my skin

leaving behind drops of their existence:

a speckled biography, melted.
i feel the sound it creates;
in each there is a special song.

the sun lays down her hands.
i dream in length
& am blanketed.

arthritis

the joints
creak:　　old hinges
　　　　　rusting together;

the locked jaw:
numbers scratched
　　　　　　　from the dial;

the elbows turn in
on themselves;

　　　　　　the knees,
original, though wooden,
　　　　　　　　& swell
in the humidity,
which　　　　　then waterlogs;

the ankles　　　rub bone
　　　　　　on bone;

the fingers become
wilted leaves
　　　　& curl
　　　　　　into the palms

things

there are things
that put us

apart

from other things

*

things happen
in process

a solution
to end all

things

*

we collect
things

to become

bigger things

removal

after finding out i might lose my feet

i touch
& am considerate.

my feet (maybe)
release from post:

so long nails
hazards to my socks;

goodbye toes,
elongated stones;

drift away heels

& ankles,
your strength pending.

*

there is an argument
on how to sew

& what stitching?

thread?

battle

temporary assistance

assist in
assisting me

*

i peel back
the hollow
black

like a sheet
there are bedbugs

or a multitudinous of creatures
disclosed

*

a nightlight

warrants

the dark

us break-up

my adjectives
are being

wild

*

he saw me yesterday
with an adverb

*

the conjunction says:

"either you stay or
you go"

*

i break away from
my verb

*

choose a new noun:
ryan, magnolia,
or hammer

thesis

stumble

you don't

though holding on

your way

on your knees
pretending
to

forgive me
or love me

neither of these
are taken out of them
as remarks

or context

neurosis

i deliberate

on a deliberation:

what is there
to oppose

twice
the contradiction

*

to mull
over seriousness

to dilute
thought

to dilate
the process

to coerce it
wide

open

*

bringing forward
after resignation
the conversation

is cynical

*

i chafe the places
on my tongue

(as it skids
across
my taste buds)

where my voice
existed

only my ears
abide
to listen

the gray

i woke to a prolonged roar

(inside my television)
paper mimicked birds;

sheets flapped aimlessly—

there is a gray fog lifting.

people reverted into spooked deer:
they scramble through the haze.

their vision transferred to outstretched arms.

oxygen became precious.
the sun became obsolete.

*

some come from the innards,
alien: layered in a different skin.

unsure of the world,
the weight of their mind
crippled them.

they touch but are unable to feel.

they only know the past;
the future is behind subterfuge eyes.

glass

just listen to the ticking
the clock caught time chasing the second
beneath the watch's monocle

*

behind the (which the moon
is wrapped within) windowpane
the man suffocates

*

the woman is extended
over the hourglass:
her skin, then fitted

the outside rain body

"sorry, no, you're beautiful."

   the clouds are perched,
   waiting. there is always waiting.
"i wait for you," anxious, paranoid:
   you will lose
   yourself; you will lose me.

   the rain tastes everything;
   licks until you're covered
   with a soppy wet.

what if you run further into the storm?

my tongue wants to polish you.

"my tongue wants …" i am inspired
   by the way you appreciate.
   i do not appreciate; not that i don't evaluate.
"… to polish you."

bushes

there is a way to watch the grass
properly.   my mother extracts them
from under her younglings,
breaking their small spines
away from their imbedded feet,
then piles them in mass graves.
                    infants—the green threads
ravel around their necks & strangulate.

all day she yanks and complains:
"i've never seen grass grow
so fast."   she sits cross-legged,
the sun paints her face.
                    she plays
gardener, aid, life support
until the last violator is displaced.

river mouth poetry

my poems are threads
sewing together
the manuscript. words
that form a portrait; a memoir.
i can't swim in the river i cry,
therefore i drown.

its
fast flowing current
didn't know what to do.
i was inhaled into the river's mouth.
tasted, swallowed, regurgitated:
my corpse lay on the bank
mangled—white petal.

smokescreen; inkblot

he is untasteful.
one-hundred blinks to clear the eyes
& he still does not
see: my love for him is iridescent.
whole, yet broken. scattered
to float like stars & lost. eventually
will we be found
together? tied or twisted?

does his mouth make sense?
his words tangle
with his reactions. i do not understand
his detachment.
he does not understand how love can be fugitive.
one moment indescribable & the next captured.

the funeral sermon

rickety, the old man
pauses;

(a memory which holds no recollection
materializes
then quickly trickles from his mind.)

like a tree in the wind,
he quivers: breaks down
in winter & creaks from the cold.

the flakes decode secrets
upheavaled from under his skin.

he lies in bed, soft as a jellyfish.

the sheets are a first layering
of burial. earth ascends to his chin.

his eyes are moons
lost in space. their orbits,
decorated. dreams of dreams of dreams:

nothing.

a house built within him
with many futile floors. rooms burst
with ugly lamps & broken souvenirs;
dust & mold & webs with dead spiders.

the black lady

charred, skin flakes
like old wallpaper.
her inner walls are baring:
ruby red grapefruit.

process & finale

i masturbated today
as you reached outside me
& we broke & i screamed
& you tasted me as rigorous—
i washed your mouth—

i grew a child
in a foreign coffin—beating,
skin marked the stretching
as trenches: a war of flesh
lashed out against the body.

i held you & we coiled together.
our exterior molted & the soft
under tissue fused & hardened again.

leukemia

the blood ate from his body
wrapped in radiation.

a hummingbird takes shelter
in his mouth; his lips
embrace the nectar that his tongue
spills out. still nothing new.

still the body caves in
onto itself. still there are
little whispers to find the sick
dying, & the sick are dying.

the worms detect his eyes,
the sparrows discover the worms.

he discerns things landing on his cheekbones.

a mother incubates her eggs inside his brain
& they are to hatch as he is
to die.

our secret argument

chains hold me down.

i regain
myself:

in the dark

(walls
i cannot see

do not block
me); indented

ankle, rust vines
up my leg:

the weight of steel
strengthens

*

my sight is laden
with abstract
conclusions

*

i relinquish myself to ink

i swim in the great black sea

i soak into the crest

i relax in the clearing

i create distorted inkblots
on the beach with my feet

nevertheless, images tumble from my body

i write with pleated ambition:
the squids are dried in the sun
& served as sugar cookies

*

my comfort is only as lithe
as my surroundings

i convert into the only thing acceptable:
a marshmallow

*

i lay in the ball field

the clay
lets my whole body
unveil its nakedness

& i allow the seagulls
to pry back my eyelids

& to untie my tongue
from my throat

i found you these

i dabble
in dabbling

the small
becomes
large

but stays
insignificant

*

"do you have
allergies?

i confiscated these
from the golden sea.

the mist tasted gritty,
seedy. the wind was permeating."

*

i'm too poor to purchase a bouquet

or even a flower

"so here is your bundle
of weeds."

poem

i spent my thoughts knowing
but could never produce

*

the blades paper-cut me
while i walk bare feet to the sturdy statues
the sculptor has created:
i observe the free art gallery

*

i am a widower to the poem

*

there are meanings
the pen scratches
into your face

*

caution: imagery may be intense

*

the man's breath is a wisp of smoke

hickory chips burn inside his stomach

*

the lady who speaks broken english:
i escort her outside; we drive;
i let her taste a tree:
"feel" "have" "know" "suffer" "undergo"

she was too numb to scream
her tongue collected her teeth

she gave me two white stones;
she pocketed the rest

we made glass in broken love

*

some girl was born
with a jughead

filled with the dead twin

before harvest

i'll eat
their finger
prints

before they're
harvested:

the raw flesh
is chewy:

i tenderize
the skin
between my teeth

it pulls apart
at the grain

readaptation

1

i've seen you outlined.
before, when there was
only a lining of skin,
not yet able to set my lips
on a foundation. i watched
your creation; the sculptor work:
his reincarnation of adam;
you were the first of his product.

i selected you as mine,
your details & your flaws.

2

your skin is soaked with chamomile.
assembled like a quilt, your stitching
hides within the body. your eyes,
removed from my mother; your smile,
i cut & paste from my sister;
your hands are from my father: worn
& worked, they operate my body
into overtime; your chest, i confiscated
from my athletic brother; though your legs
i found at the county morgue.

3

i am the eve
that generates life.
the mother. i am
the selector,
the breath, the
heart. i am
the widow-maker & then
the taker of the widow.

part two

of too much was our talk

x

the way you lived after you died

i help you pick pieces of your face
off the floor, the smaller fragments
harder to find. i crawl under
the bed, one of your eyes had rolled   .
beneath there. you smile at me
with half a lip & slurred, you reassure
in as whole a voice as possible
that "i'll be okay, daddy loves me in a way
which is hard to explain" & "thank you
little man for your support." after we make you pretty again
we play silently in my room until the stars
dry from the ruins of the house & i sleep
in a world where mommy doesn't get sad.

the years were stitches & bruises & sunglasses
then you became the woman who outgrew
gluing herself back together. you were tired
of living in a fishbowl & escaped
& swam against the current & birthed
into an avant-garde creature & given a new flesh.
you spoke the voice of birds & sang & sang
until the trees held you & you understood it was safe.

wrecked

you taper off.
& then i am nothing you understand.

your smile made your face
a stain-glass window but otherwise
it is a dirty sheet of glass

maybe you have fought with yourself
& it is blood in your eyes

your hands break into pottery & dust.

why can't there be anything easy.

i shift in my tears. maybe your hands
broke on purpose, maybe it was this way
all along, a simpler way to let go.

i've fought with words
& all you do is question

you catch my ears of fire

we are both stubborn

there are ways i used to succeed
though lately love is a puzzle
with too many pieces & we lost some

& the picture is incomplete
so we're wrecked & are wreckage

scattered at different angles of degree

we become autumn

we become mulch

we become each other

moon bleaching

i sample the pool's water with my toe.
the nip gets me drunk.

(the moon's yellow face is luminous.
she musters the arousal of men.

the pale beauty is translucent yet fervent.
she lets fingers chill on the skin of her body.

as hours dawn she swims to the edge,
escaping into the focus of the night.)

i lounge on the patio & ferment,
to let the darkness bleach my skin.

martini recipe

infuse

two parts ying

separate yang

skin the heart

the poet in the photo

a stunning young man.
very beautiful in feature.
i did not know him, or do not,
i only have a photograph,
the taken date & a name.
i am not sure if he's deceased
& though if he is alive
i cannot tell you the identity—
he may read this & know
i am speaking about a youthful him
over 40 years ago, when i was not yet born,
or thought a possibility because
neither of my parents were yet conceived.
the photograph is a replica
printed in a book. the page
i flip to so often & admire
is his casual sitting, hair draped, slantwise,
over his forehead, a sun touching him gently,
his eyes catching something aside
the camera. his delicate smile
deliquescing my reality, so i let it
bring me into his era
& i assist in the removal of the sweater,
then puncturing through his mouth
with my tongue & no one sees us.
we are straddled, one on top the other;
in his lap, my legs wrap around his waist.
his eyes are happy; his fingers
are paper cut from his poems.
he is not yet who he will be.
he will never know me.

when the weight has grown heavy

each light
is like the snow that had fallen:
every flake
has dissolved: a panel
inside her brain has become sodden.

"my memory is televised
in fragments," she said, matter-of-factly,
even though it took her three tries to finalize.

there was something small
playing in her larynx; the child-thing
retained words. a few, however, escaped,
so all you heard were bits
& pieces & nothing.

in her speech was replete.

each flake of snow chilled
a touch of skin. they were frail
but not soft & their tininess
made them treacherous.

they bonded which buried her mouth
& then her voice became ice & the heat
from her body began its melting
& the avalanche consumed her.

the impotent day

time teethed through the day
bitching, bitching, bitching—
unlike a dog, i could not get her calm,
the howl became incessant.

be like glass, he said,
but did not finish or that was the thought,
leaving me indecisive.

so i put her down.

of too much was our talk

i spoke to him,
with whoever
him
must be, though i needed
him to listen
just if briefly. i may
speak to him furthermore
if need be,
he'll allow me.
we spoke
like water, passing
everything
nothing dammed us.
it must all be important
he said
love, religion, birth, death,
the way i breathe.
you studied my lips like maps
hoping to see in advance
as to where i'm going
but nothing can give clues
because i, myself, don't know,
am lost. "i have no answers,
just questions. endlessly
as the sea. the sea that breaks
& mends itself,
lisping with a limp."

a father

your head is rolled
in oil & caught aflame
like a torch; now
i can see you from the far away
where you usually are
out of reach

woman who spoke only

i am a fragment

i am so incomplete
i do not even have a period
to denounce my ending

i am barely a quarter of an image

people judge me as inept

your mouth spoke its way to the eyes

my sister's eyes turned pearl.

rolled to the back of her head
& glazed, like a possession,

her jaw would not unclench her teeth.

the joints hardened
& the tree that saw her through the window
became jealous of her beauty:

how her limbs curved with elegance.

she shifted in the invisible wind
& our mother held her so she'd not blow away.

soon she became loose again & it rained.

psyops leaflets

i've heard the percussions
percussion
as the words break from your tongue
hard & rough. automated.
you are enormous by the sound of discharge.
something swelled inside
ready to burst & explode the whole of your body
but you spew out the gunfire
to save yourself to save what little
you have left
however the process may occur:
you detach. things begin to be eliminated
until you are singular
& your clip is emptied.

transmigrate

the plundering inward. "to
open," mouth's the handicap. hesitation.

somehow involved, there is the throat:
the entrance that insulates the trapped—

in the end (to die.) words are diminutive.

the man in the lonely room

i lust to taint your sexuality.
to delineate with my fingers the lines
of your tattoos. to kiss the inked
skin, the designs that imbed
in your arms, in your chest:
their mouths whisper to me with ambition:
to read your body then taste the definitions.
next, to forge the barren zone, above
your waistline; the snowiness
of your stomach. the demeanor of your hands,
i pretend, accommodate the subtle breaths
for me to trespass beyond the band of pants.

die doktor

doktor
you fall in love with my symptoms
dance with me like a scalpel
across the floor we make incisions to open the boards
worms & weeds & rot scour beneath
where inlies my heart, a wet dark sack.

doktor
my iron lungs transfer the chemical
to shrink my already shrunken brain:
you extract my sickness, a cesarean,
out my nasal cavity, to study the devil,
to secure in your hand a power.

doktor
you leave my body to cure
or to cure.

(to my mom)

i remember the story my mother repeated once
about her bastardized father, about how grandma
was pregnant & he forced her onto the floor,
his weight on top of her, i don't imagine she ever struggled,
taking a wire coat hanger he modeled into a hook, ramming
it inside her vagina like she was clogged,
trying to evacuate the garbage
so he could plunge his cock
into her & not have to worry.
i wondered if grandma screamed like a dying rabbit?
i remember how mom told us that crazy woman stayed
        with him.
when my mother was born
he named her after a whore he'd fucked
in mexico: aelena—now that i think about it,
it does have that spanish flavor lining the tongue.

xx

my body as youth

my hair is thinning. my eyes depend
on lenses. my noise is feeble.
my ears no longer understand sound.
my lips have shriveled, small & weak.
my mouth is still scared
to eat. my neck has almost given up
its strength. my shoulders lug around dead weight.
my elbows burn like a gas stove.
my wrists tunnel into my hands. my fingers are cracked
at each bend. my heart
is wrapped in onion. my lungs have been beaten
beyond repair. my stomach is no more a victim
than the tongue itself. my liver has always been
a failure. my kidneys compete like strangers.
my intestines are knotted with agony.
my bladder has no hold, lets it all go.
my colon stores without payment.
my penis is slack. my ass sags.
my hips are on the verge of displacement.
my thighs still contain proof of stretched skin.
my knees are crippled as are my ankles.
my feet are islands sinking. my toes are their navigator.

"i find that he did commit the offense"

after being found guilty of a write-up,
to which they had no evidence, & i was innocent.
(i spent 90 days in solitary confinement.)

i take my tongue
from my mouth—
it is dispensable.
as far back
as the teeth will reach,
i gnaw through the muscle.
the whole chunk of it
leers from between
my two-finger
blood-bathed grip.
i throw it to the floor.
maybe ants will have more use of it.

second grade: hell & honey

i hung from the back of that chair
like a gentleman, without complaint,
& i concur: my eyes felt as though
they were going to pop
but it was a strange addiction
that world between life & death,
to which i wore
the key around my neck,
& then i was found.

it was all lingo: english, panic, love;
my brain had already prepared me for death
& i was numb to sound,
sensation. i was almost gone.
was almost to the edge of beauty,
a man of love & honey.
my almost-killer had shown me a place
i have not yet found to exist.
they revived me so that i could become this.

for the lover of flowers

one night i tried dying.
the lake mirrored the signal
on the tower. the red steadily
blinked like a heart monitor.
the nurse told me i was lucky.
i laughed, denied her allegation, then cried. one night
i pretended to crawl back into my mother's
womb so that i could be
aborted. sometimes death tastes funny.
sometimes life won't let go.
the stars bleed into the darkness. the moon is
    a hunk of coal.
i stare into the light but it is the wrong light
& it does nothing. i held your hand
because i thought you loved me;
those games are better left
for the sane. i prayed to god
though he too has yet to take me.
i make a list with what i can obtain
but scribble out the ways
that scare me. in the end
i am left with none.

quota

death-lure: a silent feeding
in the lone of watery darkness
& to fall overboard: let every splash
be a hand one cannot grasp:
the boat floats as tombstone.

*

he dug his fingers into the surface
only to grab more water. it coaxed him under,
like a blanket & sleep
tucking him into the muck
to help him dream
but the images materialized liquidy & only nightmares
would become his subsidiary.

at the x

this noise is stuck. a feral
s hissing from my ear—
not a snake, a leaking
of air: "please madam
bring me back a t
to plug this sound."
it's taking me to the brink
of my o, like the owl of
insomnia; that jagged little light
from the moon that finds your un-
z eye. i hunch back
in my c & wait for the lady
to deliver me my consonant
& contemplate this u & g
someone is reading about.

spring comes in a miscellaneous shower of stars

kerosene dribbles erratically
from the leaky little rust holes
& flames drop in through the skyline
just somewhere beyond
the clamoring dawn.

everyone knew

i wore a layering
of you like a number on my arm.
everyone knew
i had sat in the fire of you;
that you reached inward
down my throat & garnered
parts of me in exchange
for parts of you;
that when we were finished
you ignited, breath lifting
into ash, cohesive,
& rooted inside my pores,
staining my skin.

by-product

they diced it into smaller pieces
before they released it
into the bin. they uprooted it from me
like it was a sin. i saw it spill out
like vomit,
the pungency of this i never wanted.

only tourists

florida was on fire one year;
we didn't know where,
we just seen the smoke lifting its huge dark arms,
reaching for the tender
& smelled the burning,
heavy as from the crematorium.
we cruised the opposite direction
along the coast. the mixed breeze
brought waves to our ears.
we drove lazily listening & reminiscing
until the road met the interstate
& left as we came, only tourists.
we heard that the ocean
relinquished the flames, that it burned
so hot some beaches turned to glass.
yet, we could never be too sure about the facts,
as i mentioned, prior,
we were only tourists.

asleep but not oblivious

out this tiny window
there is water   intense
in its reflection.

                a mirror of grand
illusion seeps upward like a maiden.

she steps
naked, pixilated
onto the shore.

her body, an exotic aquarium.

captured:
a sunfish swims behind eyes.

her whisper is inaudible.
placing his hand into hers
they both dissolve.

to watch with the intent of a blind man
is to pretend things do not become habit.

reality is reciprocating.

blink

wet the eyes

see clearer

the zone of war

there is a legion
of hibiscus

hiccupping petals

releasing a spillage
of colored flak

in a war-zone

of blustery insipid
leaves

glory in the flower

in hunger
you breach existence
& purr

naked as birth
i extend topside
dressing you with skin

you furrow into me tenderly
& we roll & ascend

your breath is sticky
like everything has perspired
& the sweat clings
to your lips

the salt
is an essence
to performance

complications of the heart

the ribs goad my organs
but there is no pipes, no music.
the only sound is the incongruous pinging
& gnashing.

the shoulder unhinges from the rotary cup
& all the trivial muscles shred & begin
to collapse on themselves until the elbow
falls loose, an unkempt pendulum.
my wrist numbs, paralytic & melts
into a dough of skin.

pain takes a needle thread with fire
& tries to fix me; our irreconcilable differences.

girl with the moth eyes

she's enthralled with staring into the sun:
playing with the shadowed orb thereafter.

how it will end

there is a repossessing

words
break & scatter

devolve
back into syllables

sounds
deteriorate
into letters

become a non language

confuse the tongue

he notches lightly
forward

catching the tamed
untamed
foreign

handwriting

as if it were
a young woman

he touches
observingly

exciting him

the body brooding
in his palm

stands & listens
then dances
& comes undone

into its preexisting
form

trickling through his fingers

tumbling into the void

the mother

she had not bled.

she lay there
like a stuffed animal
that lay
in my niece's bed:

so still, so silent.

she lay there hardbound
in her death.

her eyes black
as the night she perished
that looked to find
but found nothing.

the body

my mother was given an eviction notice
which in turn she tore into confetti & it transformed
to ash & gave her uterine cancer, then laughed
because she could no longer reproduce
so she took the broken fragments from her body & laid
them out in order & ate what death would never take
& gave what she already had a chance.

[cento]: self-exam

definition of terms:
1) turn to open   2) (insert bomb here)
3) don't have lingering doubts

they knew what they wanted:
beasts
       & violins
shall be released
against last will & testament
but tonight no music will serve
the happy majority

the visitor

he fondles
to ignore:
let's assume
his skin
is sacred.
lets breathe over his body
warm wind
but serene
& dumb.
he shuts his eyelids;
lets dominate
the kingdom
lets feed
from the harvest—
though under us
he is rotten
yet we'll savor him
nonetheless
being use
to nothing else
& soon
know
he will be in bed
with another
who enjoys the flavor
of reissued flesh

the curse of the lady who became the first rose

roots encompassed her like a wooden python
wresting her down-to-earth like a crippled animal.
her skin began to wilt & rupture:
her body knew no other way to deflate.
rigorously her blood petaled red & lammed outward;
her bones protruded as jagged spiry thorns.

grotesque picturesque

sometimes we sit on the bed
while i read. your face peering up,
froze with that smile. the day, white,
in the background. the flowers, luminous, bowing
at your feet. you are always in the forefront.
other times i kiss your too small lips.
here & there i fail you but in the end
we come back as circles.

blue beating

with all the beating
heart to artery to vein
blue birds thudding
miniature pumps
inside their chests
so fiercely as fleeting
danger, thunderous
as a bottle rocket
& pop, the small booming
against the sternum
like hands against glass.
the blood is injected
like gas, the wings burn
the wind.

how to be seduced by the moon

the yellow moon
presents herself across the floor
nude & luster. you touch her light,
the shapelessness
extends across the corners
of your hands.
you can almost hear her giggle.
she ripples in the movement of the curtains,
darting around, inching
thicker & thicker to your bed;
into your bed. you sit inside her wholeness.
she envelops you & reaches in
the leg hole of your boxers.
her painted fingernails prickle your skin.
she pushes on your chest to lie down
& whispers that she wants to watch
you masturbate. you peel off your boxers
& she flushes all over your crotch.
the gentle warmth feels like her mouth
& you are prominent.

the homoerotic romance

chisel
& not so many words

     debunk   disbelief
let it alter   something

a removed spleen   living through the pharmacy

a dribble of mustard on the goat-tee
paint the napkin   let the sun
     set the color   on ordained
yellow

     askew
the mind is about to rupture
tie it down   tie it down
it has become a monster

let the widower commemorate his loss
there is no other way to surmount

behave   every good dog is a bitch

rejoice in the joyful   then become real

if you love it let it go   a bullshit
quote to make the sorry bastard
less sorry   less of a bastard

this is when the message really matters
propaganda propagate

sell the napkin as a heart

xxx

love suffocates

a layering of dust:
a second shell: your skin

tremors:
it expels:

polarizing: i become
the content of a capsule

you swallow:
i spread within your blood

stream through
your body:

hallucinogenic: you believe
you appreciate forever

*

hearing sound
regulate: your mouth

tampers with vocabulary:
restraining words:

*

you don't feel
anymore: i break

down: love
handcuffs:

brings you in: an
interrogation

where you pretend:
memorizing lines:

where is it:
the heart

revert

people
are light: weight:

(water
residue: something
floats

across the tear
in my eye: a raft
from a broken
dam

plunges off a cliff):
paint the moon:

      the sun is plotting
      against us: his
        arm outstretched:

      we halt: we
      have come too far:
        now we will reverse:

      revert:

in the morning i advance

you're lined
   in a dream—

an earthquake
agitates
(a fracture

around my brain)

the blue glass:
is the atmosphere
that sustains
   my imagination

it keeps
my writing
together   a balance
        a flow

a reservoir

you call home
you sit there
     glancing at

the fracture
widen into a night
& you touch
what cuts

a loneliness
oozes
from your wound

it spills clouds

& disrupts
vision: a fog

thick as colored
water floods
& submerges us underneath:

we become a coral:
houses:
your lips
separate, bloom,
&

you try breathing like a fish
but drown—

resistance:
i close my eyes
& see you alive.

wolf-man

i reek my skin:
flay. the heartbeat
is a strange
disaster. it is an owl, lost
in a naked uninhabited
forest.
the quiet intensifies the rhythm.
i stalk the full mooned animal
& am
his transformation: the shedding
reminds me of a snake. the screams: the echoing
through the skeletal trees.
the wolf mutilating his human
exterior. the self is dreaming.

tollbooth

I)
we could never be
comfortable. you can
always leave the sheets
untouched. i'll
sleep elsewhere.

the night is sprinkled
through the curtain's holes.
there is a haze
that smudges my perception.

II)
you, an establishment—
a tollbooth resides
at your hands. i pay with skin.

you listen with your mouth.
your tongue withdraws
my lips.

III)
you extract my heart
from the coal
& decipher it.

sin eater

your red hair
is the fire that drives me—

i reach in
to your pants
& retrieve your cock—
i hook it:
there is no resistance—

i palm your skin
transferring differences—

your weary eyes are discs:
they glow in the excitement
from interest & try to resist—

i collect your thoughts
before i eat your sins—
there are places
where i have advantages—

i pace myself

the greenman

there are flowers
that grow from your mouth.
    they rip
your lips, your smile
widens—
your teeth glimmer through blood,
    small stones
in a red river. they touch your eyes
& taste your lens: tender,
they are vulnerable. your irises
smear under the pressure.
    your skull fractures
& blooms. roots grow
from your nostrils. your body
becomes large leaves.

the way that there is love

there is a laceration
in the factory
of your fracas
lips. i cannot
take you there—
they have closed
their doors & laid
everyone off.
the heart
is a crunchy
& bitter radish.
your eyes are dulled
marbles. your teeth
are flat concrete pebbles
that grind
against the tongue.
your mind
is an empty parking lot
that i've filled
with lost & wanted posters.
the gate, at the entrance,
is busted & swings
open letting in
waste (which have been
all the people
that come after me).

i will not identify

muse:
i scour your face
for directions, the soft
features take over
like a tide, peacefully
filling my page. your love for me
is a lie, but the pretending
is so beautiful.
i try to win but the resistance
is a dam & i am
waterlogged. there is a rock
inside my chest. it is heavy
on my lungs. i sink
to the underbelly
where the scavengers will eat
my emotions & my skeleton
will dance in the current.

closure

you are somewhere
& i am aware
of the statistics—
it is plausible
that you will not
return. you will hold
open your hand
to the world & like leaves
disappear to the earth.
forging, you will never
repeat the love
that you ran away from.

dead sea eyes

there's a need for space
to be between
               your face

&
mine ...

i'll bite your bottom lip

i want to raise blood
from your skin

i want you to realize
my sanity is
frail

i want you to taste
your failures
on my tongue:

please, space,
as i
unravel;   i weave
a web of water:
the dead sea
drips from my eyes.

what the thought of glass shows me

the landscape
is a lush
sea rolling & their leaves
are sails
catching wind. there is a forward
momentum that floats
like a kite
licking the sky: it cleaves
a cloud. the inside spills.
an infinite amount of hands
turn over & cup
the blood. they bring their palms,
filled, to their faces:
quenching, after the drought, the mud
fills in the cracks.
their bodies are wet pottery.
clay drippings build behind them.
glass breaks into feet.
they are children to be completed.

clasp

i take away from your fingers
a part of you
you'll never get back:
i want to keep you
like a charm on my wrist
to show you off
yet keep you close enough
that i'll never lose you:
you'll be mine
until i replace you:
i'll replace you only if you
become defective:
you'll only become defective
if i let you:
i will never let you.

there is a death somewhere

i'll love you
until there is a reason
to leave, though i'll drown
before you can save me.

can you take me home
& resurrect me? lips
connect like a clasp
& inhale. my heart
is a water heater:
the cold infuses
death. i exhale a geyser.
a flash flood.

it sweeps you away
before the light touches
my eyes. i'd rather you kept me dead
than to live without you.

like we've seen it

i am breaking
all the rules:

i let you bound
me with cords.

i am sat against a wall.

your hand
grips your cock.

you push your shaft between my lips,
scraping teeth.

the heat of your skin
tastes silvery.

the length
causes me to gag.

my throat is dammed.

when you pull out
saliva stretches across

like a bridge.

you shove back in
before i catch my breath

continuing to jackhammer my face.

in time
things bloom from my mouth.

xxxx

the remnant

of where we were once:

i track you. lone & sitting,
speaking against the wind,
your words are like birds: a spirited axis.

the last of the seagulls vacate
before dusk; they loosely scramble
down the beach before launching
into flight from their miniature
runway.   you are a wanderer.

you have wandered into the twilight
    again.   the sun
dips into another openness.
i come unnoticed alongside you.

fingering your fingers i interlock ours together
& try to see what you see. *what do you see?*

the intelligence comes out like blades of grass
sprouting weeds multiplying with bees
her lips break & bleed & recede into decay
into fertilizer her eyes seep honey
her nares bloom orchid like worms they crawl
up her face & she strains to breathe

"they're trying to take my eyes," you cry.
all-of-a-sudden i materialize into an image:
the protector against your invisible army
of enemies. i become more than human.
& then as if there never was anything
or never a me, the docility

gone into the sea, the current forces you underneath.

your voice, a doldrums murmur
drowned by the waves trying to lick
our feet. maybe it is curious

maybe it wants to understand or maybe
because it's newly dark it wants to make sure
we are still here. however, it cannot reach us.
pulling back, maybe we have dissolved.

you are languid in my arms. i carry the smallness
of your body back to the bed. you have liquid eyes.

you pull me close to you & whisper that they're
trying to drink your voice. your face disentangles
allowing your features to fall away. your skin thins
& modifies into blank paper. you will never be completely
filled. the ending of you will always be inconclusive.

leaving in five steps

to hell with sound

sight & smell
taste & touch

the skin is a rind
to which you'll peel back
in one layer

to expose the fruit
of indignity:
a scrap of meat no longer sweet,
the pulp spills out like sand.

the redolence will be the bitter reminder.

fumble with the weight of your tongue
or just decide that speaking
is better left unsaid.

i
try & retrieve what little
there is: the kiss
tastes abandoned. a copper lining
outlying the lips.
a coolant's pumped between
so that you cannot feel
my affection. what lingers will soon be dissolved.

there will eventually
be a lapse in time. an erasure put to your mind.

earache

my ears bubble & pop:
an underwater
sensation: semi-
deaf & a man on a whistle
is nonstop blowing:
turn the hurting
down: the eardrums
bow with reaction:
i lay back, two pillows,
close my eyes & retreat
into my mind: inside
the tomb of imagination:
the only place i can escape.

compass

in walking the driveway
i find
a puddle of broken sea:
your reflection
looking, your skin glimmers:
a bug breaks your face
swimming opposite from me

i see i am alone
your images ripple
scattering my mind

the sky's whisper
sounds like your name
i look ahead & turn
the dirt, gravel, clouds
all begin to be
you when you were you

yet now different
an alien to my eyes
maddened by what's inside
it reaches out
& takes hold like a puppet
covers your face
with an evil mask
& you are lost in purgatory
between worlds

your reality spins
like a compass
located on the pole
lost at direction
& confused

your eyes sporadically dart
in your head
it looks as though
you're not able to wake
from this nightmare

the weeds that reside in my toes

you stood
& left me standing
 i ran
but the vines
caught & tangled me
 the garden
doesn't even
forgive me
 they
held me down
& helped you
get away
  people found me
barely planted
 my face & toes
were sprouting
 i've not been
watered
barely alive
& forgetting
to breathe
 the bees have flown somewhere
& all that's left from the butterflies
are their dust
 people pulled me from the garden
like a patch of weeds
& put me in a bag
to resign
to decompose

the face of the girl behind the scarf

going through space
in my homemade rocket suit
the moon to my left
he smiles as i pass
i swim in this frantic sea
starfish glow fluorescent
shoal of rockfish swirl
curious of my alien origin
i see sunlight, bending around earth
the heavy green & blue, her makeup
underneath the white streaks of wrapped cotton
like a woman with a scarf
she hides her pretty face

ignoring the perish

a man by the wall
not noticed. a bush
growing from concrete.
his body moves, limbs
caught in the wind:
a subtle shake, an arm falls,
a hand slides
from chest to ground.
his brown eyes
resonate autumn.

islands in a winter lake

ducks: a winter lake
wings overlap
forming a feather quilt
you sleep beneath bellies
slice of light infringe
whites glimmer like fish scales
eyelash fins, ropes
from the bottom reach
your fingers: fused
feet paddle
tiny water dancers
islands erupt: toes
break surface
ripened by sun
fertilized, they dehisce
into fulvous blooms

god's delight

i undress
to the texas
embers.
i stumble
with smokescreen sight
& find myself pausing
under a burning bush.

in their war

again
mountains erupt
they elope into a flame
only god can contain
        i sit in the field
        distancing myself from their war
        watch the shell-shocked trees
        lose themselves
        i keep an eye on the leaves
        bomb the ground
i listen: the wind
howls retreat
i feel remorse
the grass is forced
into scattered debris
        again
        there isn't any sense of peace
        no treaty under way
        a disorder that leavens
        a colored scar

the walls of summer

i lie
back

let my eyes
glide

above my face
a butterfly
flutters
my hand

is seen
to be plausible
a piece
to breach

a flower
to let my legs
hang over the petals
to let pollen cluster

the inside of my mind
is built with texture

the sick do not resist

him, in the corner,
spaced out
& overflowing

he moved
to the other side
letting it surface

he took
it with his teeth
& laid his head up
at the ceiling.

his eyes,
slicked with oil,
rolled, undecided,
he took a long blink
& exhaled.

med.u.s.a.

jump-start, somehow,

the battery
tapered
to my shoulders

a hammer
doesn't work
doesn't knock enough
to rattle around

a flow, a connection,
an idling process

    *

the structure's frame
is becoming
a rusted sculpture
of insignificance

no one has
any curiosity about

    *

words that were
soon appear to
disappear

fade into an abysmal
page who mouths them in
with her tongue

laps up verse
turns them into a mirage

& swallows each poem
inside her snake throat

    *

i begin not knowing

forgetting the forgotten
& forgot the forgetting

    *

my mind is stone

    *

a headlight
cracks

mary & her lamb

mary has a little lamb
its fleece, white as snow

mary takes it to the slaughter house
& watches the butcher take its soul

its blood runs red, its fleece is shed
its body hangs like a wet towel

mary had a little lamb
she takes its lamb chops home

the crow that looms in my head

table side: the lunacy is crows
feet, perched aloft
years of nothingness & retreat:
it skews a self: the bigger
half too heavy: the smaller,
a loon man countenancing
the sea: fish
rampant, suckling his leg hair:
wings fan over eyes:
a depression: a feathery
blind that loathes the pills,
enshrouded as trifling candies:
a momentary relapse of satisfactory:
the crow absconds & borrows
pieces of me: he returns
rotund

a history of past romance

we stroll in the grass: barefoot:
strands weigh
beneath feet: few sprout
between toes: we lay down a blanket:
we lie backside underneath cotton overlay:
we peek from holes: blue
ceiling: our gender
equivalent: only our outer dimensions
variate: how easy
to get lost: eyes descend:
hands become men: enforcers:
our bodies become a battlefield: i
succumb to you: the sun
photographs us: a history
that will become omitted
by decisions we deem
understandable: years: lovers:
the fringe under clouds
became nothing more
than clouds themselves

the man & the pendulum

sprinkling: i pursue clamoring
from inside a public shower: the water
distorts their words:
i am irrelevant: they are
men: one is kneeling:
the water coaxes his eyelids together:
the man standing
repeats himself: the other's head
is a pendulum: his thick hair
is filled with fingers: the other's
breathing fluctuates: his abs
flex: he clutches the man's face
to his pubic mound:
the kneeling man gurgles:
liberated: apparently swallowed: ascending:
they dry: dress: depart
separately

skin chiseler

toes curl: my soul
detaches:
pleasure: it rips my breath
away: massage
points of passion: i convulse: hold
my skin to my body:
you exorcise me from past lovers

the old man: his sparrows

the yard: (the sparrow
unsowing seed)
is balding: thinning
in areas where blades
remain (filling
his stomach with productivity):
he allows them
to feed from his scalp: loneliness
prevailed: fracturing him:

becoming venerable
he whittles trees:
letting rivers flow
through his fingers: he
only cries
when the sparrow sleeps:
scared: his empathy
utters to him: you will drown
the tiny birds otherwise:

he glimpses
when they are preoccupied:
fearful
he may be deserted:
he yields no reason
to panic them: their comfort
is an alibi to breathe

lung cancer

yesterday concludes: apathy
possessed my life: fetched
psychosis:
miniature psychotic episodes:
voices insist i write this: voices
pretend i don't exist: do i really
want this: what do i
want: which is the poet:
the body or the voices:

the visions: it is clear
on what i should see: the voices
help explain them: they have no
patience: short tempered:
occasionally i get it wrong:
it is a punishment i cannot escape:

i write to keep them abstracted:
i write to control the future:

i write: the cigarette burned
my lungs: how else will anybody
see the scars

xxxxx

animal instinct

we waited. i contemplated,
developing featherless wings
creating them as a sheath
to undermine the resistance.

my mind flies with temptation.
it is a wild caged bird
that forces itself outward.

the bird brain mutates the human self
overpowering normality.
my human eyes overcast
forming everything into visionary shadows.
my eyeballs fill with oil
transforming into black beady stones.
my mouth protrudes beakish
stretching my nose into two holes.
my voice loosens & language
becomes alien.
my teeth unhinge from my gums.
my lips harden.
my back contorts & elongates
perpendicular with my legs.
my knees invert. the caps rotate.
my bones crackle as they reverse
their movement.

you waited.

tender force of acceptance

i've disturbed you
with a kiss. my apologies.
your skin is opaque.
it creases when you frown.
your face shifts. it quivers
under the warm chill
of breath. i am a simple lover
with simple fingers
which slide through your simple hairs.
you learn to begin
to understand. you realize
it's the simplest way.

i arouse you with a kiss.
my strength. your skin is creamy.
it smooths when you smile.
your face blossoms. it becomes
rosy with the connection
of lips. you are a tender lover.

fuhrer

i'm a screaming hitler
popping through the canal
into this filthy hell—
i'm released from the womb
where i was god
into this anonymous place
of sacrificial hands—
they poke & pry & prod & touch
as though i'm extraterrestrial:
ten fingers, ten toes,
two eyes, two ears,
one mouth, one nose
... then they stop
as though disappointed
that i'm only human

balloon

i needle the cloud.
it burst, spewing sunshine,
spilling it over the outside.
some spattered in my window.

god became me

i molt:
the loam
washed away; cleansed,
the light is let
to absorb in through my pores.

god filled me, though i
was not empty.
he could scarcely fit.
my new skin, still soft,
tore & damaged.

i bled & earth drank me.
they tasted god
& confused me with him
& began to eat my flesh
like bread.

god is too far gone

i have discovered god today
hiding naked in a dumpster.

he is dirty & sticky
& feral like an alley cat.
when i attempt to kindle him
he bites at my hand with yellowed teeth.

the flies have nested in his sores.
they're dank with pus
& putrid. his toes, possibly, gangrenous.

i feel sorrowful for god
but he is lost in his way.

writing poetry

can you read
between the lines? the subtle hints
floating like a pine needle.
almost too small to the naked eye,
but there. you eventually spot it lying
under the blue line.

it lounges & confesses particles
& in time confides in you:

opens like a fist
& becomes at ease
showcasing its tender definition.

the secrets it's collected
incubate inside like pearls.

concerning the body

there's still time to shut the door, lock
the bolt, get the car engine's sound
from your mind—you are already focusing
on driving away; the gravel crunching under tires;
the rearview mirror will be the only way
you might partake the last glimpse of me;
there is still time.
put your suitcases down, anywhere,
just drop them on the floor; sit—please,
don't be hesitant; let me take your hand.
you resist, though i don't care
to beg; there's still time.
your eyes puddle, balancing
on your lower-lashes—
i hope in them there's a reference
to love; there is still time.

what bears to be born

with all the friction, creates a cloud
which manifests lightning bolts in my mouth.

the wasteland

thank you, synopsis,
for turning to the silence,
with its weightlessness
blaring like a set of wings.

the sun's almost wet.
stare into its face,
you'll see water slip
falling out of place.

i tie the leaves
on the limbs of every tree
to let them dry—
someone snips them to the ground.

toilet paper

a white lotus
poised in water.

its tiny existence
dissolving.

[sonnet]: mechanical rising

(he absorbs low-frequencies)
his tongue sponges the spilled sound:
it vibrates between the teeth
& radiates to the crown
fluctuating his brain waves
which in turn generates surge
raising creativity
to become a da vinci
or a poetic ginsberg
he's in a mind-state of craze:
his hand is a sonic-beast
scribbling across the page
& he doesn't seem to cease
the artistic inner rage.

[sonnet]: we fucked like drugs

we fucked, null, in the shower
until i bled. his huge cock
embarked through me—bore power
that i craved—his hands were locked
to imprison me. he pumped,
briskly, painful ecstasy
& i screamed & begged & felt
the great desire he dealt
like i was a whore, sleazy,
& deserving it. he cummed
in my ass a blast of cream
so hot it burned within me—
he held me in that hushed dream.
his cock softened inside me.

attempting to attempt perfidy

the weather is as delusional
as i am. spring, & snow screens the ground,
like cotton to be picked. dusty white
flakes dock on the panes of glass
& fuse into the harbor.

incorporeal america

there are 5,000 men
        hunched
around   a
        fire

they're mostly
                homeless
yet a few
lurking   businessmen
scour the edge:

there's a greasy film
to the poor. a cheap
                oil.

pinion dreams

i shuffle out in the twilight
in the dyspeptic street
tugging my dreams on a leash.
—there was a bar & i offered
to buy this young man a drink
but he declined stating
he only allowed himself one
(raising the bottle to make his point)
because he drove.
he casually sipped, like i didn't exist. —they piss
on a sidewalk that i don't bother
to clean.

in the belly

being folly in the crush
of winter; a brisk breeze
imbibes sweat: sweet
tongue of cool hews the jacket,
parts it like moth wings: the elision
of snow isn't tempered,
it is sputtered yet the snow
is a fierce father—eats his children:
tries to duplicate cronos; though unfoiled
by a stone. the face of the moon
is outlandish, as she laughs
in the corner.

[sonnet]: exile: incubating eden

i'm to the moon a dwarf star.
somewhere this tiny light sears
through the black hand of space: scar
god & his temper appears—
we're merely nonexistent:
a pin needle hole absorbs
life; backspace; our extinction:
he changed man without distinction.
filling in the eye sockets
to rescind disfigurement,
shriveling the tongue minute
to cancel all the warfare,
& making the ears acute:
life will be handled with prayer.

cocaine play

a trace of cocaine
in the crevice of nail.

you lick
my face buried in your neck.

breath burns-spins-retreats.

you laugh fundamentally.

factory

i thirst for your output:
the input of your hands.

in rae's foot-petals

after rae armantrout's "spent"

dream as in forget.

imagine as in fictitious.

imagination as in someplace
different, or not here
at present.

to dream
is to lean,
hazardously,
to one side.

have you imagined?

hazard
as in lost.

spin, & spin

i

roll

a thread
into a

ball

between
my thumb
& forefinger

& roll

a ball
into a

thread

to watch it loosely
fall

robust

urn

we place
ourselves
before the fire.
            nevertheless
there is touch
inside
this skin—

a push
to feel
the flesh:
            nevertheless
to burn
is to
conjoin.

fragment #16

i've
been in
the inner lining
of your
love

you shelf me

human
content

open my pages

dog-ear
what you prefer.

i'd like to think we were fated

as lover

though tormentor,
you are what error brings.

love poem

tender: delicate, fragile,
frail, sensitive: acute,
keen, perceptive, sharp:
cutting, edgy, ground,
jabbing, jagged, lacerating,
piercing: booming, clamorous,
deafening, earsplitting, loud,
resounding, ringing: golden,
resonant, round, sonorous,
vibrant: alive, animated,
astir, busy, lively:
active, brisk, energetic,
frisky, peppy, perky,
spirited, vital: springy,
vivacious: gay, jazzy,
pert, racy: jaunty.

the skeletons

there are places
which i have

buried. have i?

which places are there?

...

i have
scoured the skeletons

in my frame
of mind:

they interrogate
regarding
too many
truths.

i levee:

they turn & forget of my existence.

they're rapt
in their transliteration.

i observe
their babble

comprehending
the abatement
of nothing.

you are my novel

simple is at a standstill.

standoff.
            we are now

foreigners. days thin out.

weeks: silent weaponry.

you are becoming more fiction
than lover, more pretend
than real.

john thompson is a poet, blood & life. he's been writing
since 2001, but only has honed in on his talent since 2007.

he lives in kentucky, with his pet chihuahua, cricket.
he's engaged to Eric & they plan to marry 7-7-18.

he enjoys corresponding with fellow poets, & responds
to every email he receives & hopes everyone writes him
at iammisterpoet@gmail.com

john thompson appreciates everyone who reads & enjoys
his poetry & he hopes that someone can find something
positive & insightful in it.